Success w

Contents

**All drawings, including the front cover,
by Sue Ward**

ISBN 0 901687 14 6

**Consultant Editor to the Booklet Series
Tony Lord**

Acknowledgements

The authors of the booklet include Peter Thompson, who has written several books on propagation and other gardening topics, Deb Goodenough, garden manager at Osborne House, I.o.W., and previously manager of the nursery at Ventnor Botanic Garden, Richard Bird, writer and a previous editor of *The Hardy Plant* and Tim Ingram, nurseryman with a special interest in germination and Australasian plants. With Tony Schilling, who talked about seed collection overseas, they presented their work at the 'Success with Seed Day' in March 1997 at Sparsholt College, Winchester. This national event was organised by the HPS Hampshire Group.

Our thanks to all those who organised the event and contributed, directly and indirectly, to the production of this booklet – including the authors who reworked their presentations to fit the booklet's requirements, Carole Hudson who transcribed the recorded tapes and Sue Ward who drew the illustrations.

Kate Hills
Editor

Roscoea cautleyoides   **Sue Ward**

Introduction

PETER THOMPSON

ANYONE WHO INTRODUCES A BOOKLET of this sort has two options: either to steal the thunder of those who come after by talking broadly about the things they will later write about in detail, or to concentrate on a few salient points of particular interest to the introducer. I prefer the latter option.

The subjects of this booklet can be simply and concisely summed up as *keeping the seed alive and enabling it to germinate.* I hope it will help enable you to find out how to do both. Keeping seeds alive is remarkably simple. It is a matter of keeping them cool, cold in fact, and dry. Persuading them to germinate can also be remarkably simple but, as I am sure you are all well aware, it can also be extremely frustrating – with many kinds of plants it can drive you to tears.

When I arrived at Kew in the early 1960s it issued, like most other botanical gardens throughout the world, an annual seed list and, because Kew was a large and prestigious establishment, it provided a large and impressive list. Year by year the seeds of some five thousand different species and cultivars growing in the gardens were collected and duly recorded in lists distributed to other botanic gardens who sent back their requirements. Thousands of packets of seeds would then be dispatched to them to add to their collections. But time was pressing and there was little opportunity at any stage to check the quality or authenticity of the seed.

I arrived in an empty laboratory just before Christmas with only a hazy idea of what I was supposed to do. My sole guide had been the advertisement of the job for which I had applied – and I had lost that. No one else seemed to have a clear idea of what I was there for either, so something had to be concocted fairly quickly. Seeds seemed to offer a promising starting point. They did not demand too much equipment, collections of seed were available in the gardens, and they were something that could be worked on even in the depths of winter. I asked for a collection of the mint family, *Lamiaceae (Labiatae)*, from the Seed List – some seventy or eighty different species – and started looking at them.

Lamiaceae seeds are quite distinctive (like tiny nuts) and it soon became obvious that a number of the collections were not what they should have been. Some contained bits of soil, fragments of dried vegetable matter and seeds of unidentified plants of other families, but nothing remotely resembling anything attributable to the mint family. Others were flat and empty, and others were misnamed. The upshot was the discovery that less than half the packets provided good quality seeds of the species they were supposed to contain.

That involved a tremendous waste of time and effort, not just for those who collected the seed, but for those who tried to grow it too. Nor was it a problem confined to Kew. The conditions under which almost all seed lists were produced made it practically impossible to spend the time and effort necessary to guarantee the results. However, it was well known that seeds could be stored and, done successfully, that could provide a way for collections made one year to be kept alive and sent out year by year until the supply became exhausted, and another collection was necessary to renew stocks. Obviously if a seed list contains five thousand items and each can be kept for ten years, only five hundred need be collected each year – a much more relaxed operation that allows time for checking and quality control.

That was really why the Seed Bank was set up – as a means of running the Seed List more effectively – and during the early years it was based on a small cold store set up by the Gardens Department. It ran that way for several years before its possibilities as a conservation tool for the long-term preservation of seeds of threatened species was recognised. This idea was sparked off when ICI proposed to construct a reservoir in Teesdale to supply their chemical works in Middlesbrough. This led to a great deal of fuss and bother because in doing so they would inundate areas of sugar limestone and other geological formations on which grew a virtually unique flora, one said by some to have survived practically unchanged since the end of the last Ice Age. Collections of seeds were made from these doomed plants before the dam was filled, sent down to the Seed Bank, and as far as I know are still there and could be for many years to come.

What Kew did in order to set up the Seed Bank, anyone can do on a small domestic scale. The best way to keep seeds alive for a long time is to keep them cold, very cold. You cannot keep them too cold – not even if stored in liquid oxygen at -180 °C. I am not suggesting that you should keep liquid oxygen in your house or risk frostbite to keep your seeds alive. They will keep perfectly well stored in a freezer cabinet. This is better than a refrigerator not only because it is colder but because you can get away with alien objects in the freezer more easily. People open refrigerators several times a day and become irritated if they see things they suspect should not be there. So keep your seeds in the freezer – it provides an ideal storage temperature for the seeds and is better for domestic harmony too.

The other essential is to keep them dry. That is done by putting them in an airtight box (a biscuit tin or plastic container for cakes is ideal) with some crystals of silica gel. Flower arrangers know all about silica gel. It is a harmless and inoffensive crystalline mineral that absorbs water, and can be obtained from good chemists under the name of Sorbsil in the UK.

Pour a thin layer of the crystals over the bottom of the container, place the packets of seed over them and put the closed container in the freezer. Small envelopes can be used to hold your own home-saved seeds, provided the corners are sealed with masking tape to prevent escapes. Commercial seeds packed in foil can be stored as they are until they are opened; then any remaining seeds should be removed from the foil and stored in paper envelopes. When you want to sow seeds, take the

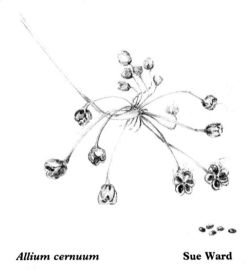

Allium cernuum   **Sue Ward**

container out of the freezer but leave it for an hour or so before opening it to warm up to room temperature otherwise water may condense on the cold surfaces of the seeds. Sow as many seeds as you need, then seal the packets with masking tape and put the rest back into the freezer. It is as easy as that and, stored in this way, seeds that would be dead within a year or two in packets in a drawer will keep ten, twenty or more years.

I will spend much less time on the topic of seed germination because it is an endless subject and one that is covered elsewhere in this booklet. There are major problems to be solved here and, if I may now climb up onto my hobby horse for a little while, they result from failing to take a broad view of seed germination. During the fifty years or so that I have been interested in seeds I believe our understanding of the processes that lead to seeds germinating – or not – has scarcely developed at all. We glibly talk about dormant seeds when nobody, as far as I know, has satisfactorily defined what that means and all we are actually saying is that they do not germinate. We list 'forms of dormancy' by categories; this reveals nothing but gives us a reassuring, though false, sense of understanding. For example, many of the clover family, including legumes and sweet peas, produce seeds enclosed so securely in their coats

5

that until these are damaged water cannot penetrate to the embryo. Obviously such seeds cannot possibly germinate until wear and tear damages their defences and they become hydrated – yet we describe intact seeds as 'dormant' even though we know they are not in a position to germinate. We also label seeds like hellebores 'dormant' because, however apparently favourable the conditions, they do not germinate soon after we sow them but only after undergoing a series of experiences months later. 'Dormant' hellebore seeds are clearly entirely different from 'dormant' sweet pea seeds but we have devised no way of defining these differences.

I also think that we should look for broader more systematic ways to relate the situations in which plants grow naturally to their germination responses. Observations tell us that seedlings emerging immediately before the onset of extreme cold or drought are likely to die; those that appear at the onset of favourable conditions are more likely to survive. So we conclude, reasonably enough, that the conditions in which plants grow impose particular restraints and offer particular opportunities, and that a plant is likely to survive only when the seeds it produces respond to what goes on around them in such a way that seedlings have at least a chance of surviving. Under natural conditions this chance may be very small. An oak tree can spend two or three hundred years producing perhaps a ton of acorns a year, yet, on average, only one acorn needs to germinate and grow to maturity to ensure the survival of the population. Gardeners, by and large, are not happy with such odds and want a higher return than one tree from hundreds of tons of acorns. None the less, looking at the places where plants grow and trying to relate them to germination can point the way to success.

I have very little space to go into this but an example can be found amongst perennials which grow in association with grasses. These grow under demanding conditions. Grasses are assertive plants, all-embracing, that dominate their environment; anything that lives amongst them survives only by conforming to their cycles of growth and development. It might seem that spring would be a good time for seedlings to emerge. A grass sward in spring is often ragged and open but seedlings trying to occupy these gaps have little chance of competing successfully with established plants with their roots packed with stored reserves in support of vigorous growth. The time when seedlings do have an opportunity is in late summer after the grasses have flowered and themselves produced seeds. Then there are also gaps in the sward and as soon as autumn rains provide enough moisture, seedlings of all kinds emerge to fill them. The result is that many plants found amongst grasses in meadows, steppes and prairies produce seeds that germinate rapidly and easily without special pre-treatments of any kind.

Alternatively, we might take a quick look at perennials that grow naturally in woodlands. Here they also grow in association with very dominant plants – the trees that tower above them – though this is an entirely different situation. Because most flower early, before the trees produce their leaves, their seed is shed around midsummer when the ground is warm and maybe moist – conditions apparently ideal for germination. However, the overhead leaf canopy is then at its maximum and a bluebell seedling, for example, germinating in deep shade during June would have little chance of survival. Unlike grassland perennials, those that live amongst trees are likely to have mechanisms which delay germination until the branches of the trees are bare, and enough light reaches the ground to provide the seedlings with the energy they need to survive.

These examples, only two amongst many, illustrate how patterns of germination depend on features of the environment that affect the chances of seedling survival. Gardeners can use them as a guide when trying to devise ways to encourage seeds to germinate and produce seedlings.

Seed or Chaff?
Collecting Seed in the Garden

DEB GOODENOUGH

IT IS GOOD TO WRITE ON A SUBJECT that one very much enjoys. Collecting seed gives me great pleasure though it also fits in with my job as nursery manager at Ventnor Botanic Garden.

My earliest recollections of gardening are of collecting seed. I grew up on a farm in Canada where we were subsistence farmers. Our garden had to feed us through the year so we grew all our own vegetables. Also, for her own interest, my mother had about two acres as a flower garden. She collected her own annual and some perennial seeds so that she could carry on growing year by year. As a little girl I used to follow on behind her collecting the seed and picking the vegetables. Usually we would go collecting on a nice sunny day and this made it all very enjoyable. I found the seed fascinating: they came in all shapes, sizes, colours and forms. Each one seemed different and, as a young child, I could relate to their smallness.

WHY COLLECT SEED?

Why do we collect seed? *Primula vialii* offers one explanation. It is one of my favourite primulas and, as a choice plant, it is always quite expensive. About nine years ago, I needed about five plants but bought just one for £3.20 The plant flowered and I collected the seed. From that one plant I had three hundred the following year. So it is a way of multiplying what we have, with limited resources. There is also that satisfaction you get in estimating their worth – 300 × £3.20! You feel as though you have cheated someone, though I'm not sure who. Another reason for collecting seed is that we often come across plants that are difficult to obtain. You are lucky if you find *Geranium palmatum* for sale but if you have one plant that means you have the potential to have more.

Then there is that potential to get something different. People question whether they should collect seed from cultivars because there is such variation but as I am not selling plants it is not a problem. I am a proponent of variety. If you sow viable seed something different might arise. You cannot predict that the offspring are going to be that particular cultivar but it is always exciting to look for new things and find something different. They may not always be good but they could, of course, be better. Species are different, of course, and will come relatively true most times unless they are quite a promiscuous genus – but you will get to know those by experience.

Then there's the fun aspect. Collecting seed in company is very enjoyable for all ages. It can be quite a social event. I used to do it by myself but as the seed list grew we needed to start a volunteer programme. This worked well as it is quite companiable work – you don't have to think an awful lot and you can chat at the same time. Choosing a nice day is essential though.

One warning about seed collecting: it can become addictive. Once you become enthusiastic about collecting seed you start looking at plants from a different point of view – not just at the flowers but at their potential. My husband calls me a squirrel because I am always looking for the seed and am getting to the point where I don't look at the flowers as much. Others may walk by fatsias, for example, and recognise that the seeds are beautiful but they may not register that they are the mechanism to grow more. Every plant has its own mechanism for distribution. I was quite excited the first time I collected seed from *Impatiens* with the seed pod bursting in my hand. Once you begin to understand these processes you can get hooked trying them out.

Saving seed means too that we are able to be generous with our plants without having to raise the extra plants ourselves. We can send seed to friends (it is a lovely present to send with a Christmas card or for the New Year) or to seed distribution schemes in neat small packets. We don't have to load our car with plants – we can send our plants easily through the post as seed.

SAVING SEED

When do you start collecting seed? Remember the basic rule of seed collecting: you have no seed until the plant flowers. So, first you look for the flowers. It is relatively straightforward with plants like species pelargoniums where the flowers and the seed are on the plant at the same time. Indeed, flowers are a useful reminder, for when they have finished it is easy to forget that you intended to grow more of that particular plant. Many plants will give you a good indication of what to collect. It is obvious that you don't collect the green seed. The seed of 95% of plants is dry and brown and you have a lengthy opportunity to collect what you need. You can come back to some like *Malope* over six to eight weeks as the seed gradually ripens off.

There are plants like penstemons and *Allium sphaerocephalon* for which you have to wait patiently. They carry their seed heads for what seem like months. They look so tatty that the natural urge is to clear them away but neatness and tidiness do not go well with seed collection. There are plants, such as *Dierama pulcherrimum*, whose seeds are very attractive but if you leave them too long you risk losing your seed source. Depending on how much seed you require, collect what you need and leave the rest as ornament. You need to be patient yet remember to check back so that you can collect it when ripe.

There are plants that leave you wondering where the seed is. After a while it becomes more evident but some plants don't give you the answer readily. Those bits that look like little twigs on *Glaucium*, for example, will ripen off eventually and split to give you seed. Only one or two of them may ripen however and then very slowly. *Robinia hispida* may only

Lathyrus nervosus   **Sue Ward**

produce one or two pods in the occasional year. So, again, it is a case of observation. When you do find them mark them in some way as a reminder to yourself to check later because the seeds may take 4-5 months to ripen. You have to keep an eye on them and get them before they are shed or the squirrels get them or someone else takes them. When working in a public garden I would patiently wait for seed to ripen but sometimes someone would get there before me. The frustrating thing was knowing that the seed wasn't even ripe.

Then there are those plants that will set seed only if the season is clement. It is not a question of 'from flower to seed' in 3-4 months; this may take nine months, depending on the weather. *Cobaea scandens* is treated as an annual in the UK but if you have a mild summer and winter it will carry on and set seed. The seed should be collected in December, or January if the weather remains mild, so you do have to be very patient. It is a short-lived perennial but if you do get it through a winter it will carry on and produce that many more flowers the next year.

Some plants such as *Digitalis ferruginea* produce copious amounts of seed. Once they have finished flowering cut down the stems or they will self-seed in their thousands. Unless you are sending the seed to say the HPS Seed Distribution scheme, two or three flower stems are usually sufficient for your own needs. Don't rely on one because that's the one that will be blown over or uprooted by the dog!

You have a very short time to collect seed from some plants: fennel for example. You don't really notice when it is flowering and it seems only to take a week for the seed to ripen and then be shed and for seedlings to appear all over the place. Keep an eye on the plants. Get to know them and know when things are happening; observation is the key to seed collection.

As you start getting to know your plants and seed, you realise that there are exceptions to the rule about collecting seed when it is ripe. *Knautia macedonica* is a very pretty plant which self-seeds around the garden. People are always asking for it so I wanted to collect seed and pass it on but, for several years running, I kept missing the opportunity. I would see the green seed but within twenty-four hours it would be disseminated. I decided to collect the seed green and, though it needed to be separated and dried, that proved the key.

Then there are the annuals and the question of whether to take the whole plant. If there are still flowers you will probably want to keep the plant as long as possible. If, however, you think you have had enough of it, you can just pull up the whole plant and put it in a bag.

When we think of flowers people often forget that grasses have flowers. Their seeds are some of the easiest to collect and germinate. Don't forget shrubs and trees as well. Although I've touched more on annuals and perennials, trees produce a great deal of seed – a cone would be enough to forest a whole neighbourhood.

COLLECTING

The requirements are simple: a pair of secateurs, paper bags and a nice sunny day. Seed collecting comes at that time of the year when a great deal is happening in the garden. You need to pick the vegetables, to tie things in and you also just want to sit and enjoy the garden. So try to minimise the work. Collect what you need and put the seed in paper bags. Store the bags open (to keep the seed dry) until you can get around to cleaning it.

Write on the bag exactly what it contains. It is so easy to convince yourself that you will remember but when you have various cultivars which resemble each other and similar varieties, you will regret not noting the name. Even if you cannot remember the correct name give yourself clues: 'the pink flower to the rear of the left-hand border'. The name may come to you later – possibly in the middle of the night – or you can consult your reference books. For your own guidance it is a good idea too to note the date. It acts as a reminder to you when that seed will ripen the following year. Every season will vary several weeks one way or the other but it starts to give you a guide to when you need to look for seed.

How much seed you should collect is a good question. With some it is quite obvious that you've collected a great deal of seed. *Hypericum* carries lots of ripe seed but there is not much in each of the little capsules and it takes an awful lot of time to collect and clean. When you are collecting you can judge when you have enough. If in doubt always collect more rather than less seed because you can always throw it out or give it away later but you can't always go back and get more.

You should collect seed when the conditions are right – the driest time of a bright sunny day. In the summer you may have from 10am until 4 or 5pm; when into September and October there are really only a couple of suitable hours. Never count on the weather. I always collect some seed as it starts to set if it is dry. You can always return later if the weather is good and collect more but in our climate you need to collect when you can. Some years are fine for collecting seed but then there are those summers when it always seems to be raining and you have no choice but to collect in wet weather. Then you will need to dry the seed off before storing or it will rot.

I have always meant to get myself a nice gunny sack to carry around as I collect paper bags of seed but I generally use rubbish bin liners. They are far from ideal for you have to dry the seed immediately afterwards. Even if you think you are collecting the seed very dry, there is still a fair amount of moisture and the seeds will sweat on a warm day with all the attendant potential problems.

You may not have the facilities of, say, Kew for drying seed but you can do an awful lot from the home base. I collect 300-500 sorts of seed and all of them, in paper bags, go into boxes which fit into my small airing cupboard which is usually stuffed full of seed packets but thankfully not all the seed matures at once. I am very fortunate for I have a very inefficiently insulated boiler and the airing cupboard is dry and very warm.

If you have seed that is damp you need to turn the seed bags around every now and then so that you get all the seed capsules drying off evenly. How long is long enough? A particular seed may take 3-4 days to a week to dry off. Don't leave them in the airing cupboard for a month but I must admit I have left seed for a couple of weeks and they have not been damaged.

SEED CLEANING

Seed cleaning can be as enjoyable as collecting. It is a good plan to collect seed and clean it that same night but often this just doesn't happen. Collecting comes at a busy time of year and the cleaning is best left to the winter months. So keep it dry. I often clean the seed when there is something on the television that doesn't need my full attention. There is the feeling of doing something gardeningwise at a time when you can't work outside, with the next year's crop at your fingertips.

Once again, the tools are very simple: a few sieves and sheets of paper. Fudge tins are wonderful because you can see all the seed and winnow it from the chaff.

It takes a while to 'get your eye in', to be able to differentiate between what is viable seed and what is not. As you sow seed, start studying it closely. Even if you aren't collecting it, start looking out for the seed and scrutinise it. After a while it becomes quite obvious. There is probably about 1-2% of which I am unsure. If in doubt I leave a lot of chaff when cleaning and sow the lot. For the most part, though, the seed becomes very obvious and you get to know the different genera of plants and even particular species. If you have a microscope you can enter a different and fascinating world in which you can acquire a lot more information for identification.

The question of how you get the seeds from fleshy fruits seems to deter people from collecting them. It is rather like jam-making. The tools are very simple: a sieve and some muslin – I have used an old muslin nappy. It is probably the least enjoyable aspect of seed collecting – the smells of bletting seed are not that pleasant as the fruit rots. The flesh prevents seeds from germinating so as much as possible has to be cleared away. Some take only a few days of soaking before they are soft enough to get the seed out; some take weeks and weeks and you need to change the water occasionally, not for the seeds' sake but for the household's sanity.

I have tried all sorts of containers for storing seed, anything from film canisters (which were very good though I often lost seed in removing the lid) to the specimen jars I now generally use. It is said seed should be kept in a dark container but it is also useful to see how much seed you have and if you can keep the container in the dark it is perfectly acceptable. In the deep freeze seed will retain its viability.

I haven't touched on fleshy seeds because that is quite another topic. You cannot readily store seeds like oak, horse chestnut, sweet chestnut and the like. You should collect them fresh and sow them right away.

TAKE CARE

Watch out for poisonous seed, such as the castor oil plant. If in doubt, wear gloves for collecting and cleaning. Although *Phytolacca* fruits are not poisonous, they can stain your hands purple so wear rubber gloves. People's sensitivities differ but there are some plants with which you know you have to take care. I collected *Helleborus foetidus* one year when it was very damp and the seed pods slightly green. I found they made my fingers numb and it took several days for the sensation to wear off. Then there is seed like rue which you have to be very careful about handling in the sun. You probably already know which plants are the ones to watch out for by the irritants in the leaves – the seed can be equally as irritant. There are also seed pods such as *Fremontodendron* with very minute hairs which can irritate. *Chelidonium majus*, the greater celandine, has a wonderful orange sap that burns the skin. It used to be a treatment to remove warts, I discovered later. A couple of mistakes and you will learn very quickly.

CONCLUSION

You can probably anticipate my conclusion: from little seeds, great trees will grow. Once hooked, like me you'll be looking at flowers for their potential for seed and the next generation of plants. I am an addicted propagator; I want to raise more all the time and although I take cuttings I find seed offers greater opportunities. Collecting fresh seed means you get very good results as 90% of the seed will be viable and you will get a corresponding good germination rate. So, happy sowing, growing and collecting.

Sowing and Growing

RICHARD BIRD

THERE WAS AN ARTICLE in the AGS *Bulletin* (Blaxman, Sept. 1996, 322-5) about a grower who was very interested in species *Viola*. In the past he had germinated them in the conventional way using pots and compost but he had discovered that he got a better germination rate by following a method advocated by Norman Deno. He sprinkles the seed with gibberellic acid-3 powder (GA-3 is obtainable from research laboratories and costs £17-plus per gram). He then places it on a numbered square of dampened paper towel. This is then folded and put in the refrigerator. Every two weeks all the seed is checked with a magnifying glass and any seed seen to be germinating is then removed with tweezers and potted up. Another grower, who was one of the best at growing very difficult high alpine plants, had a somewhat different medium for growing his plants. When asked what sowing compost he used, he replied that he used old potting compost and bench sweepings. It did not matter what, as long as it would support a seedling!

Here are two extremes of growing from seed, both very successful and yet so different. The point of this introduction is really to show that there are almost as many ways of germinating seed as there are gardeners. From the general gardener's point of view, I suspect that the methods adopted have more to do with what suits the gardener rather than what suits the seed. Seed seems more adaptable than we are.

It isn't quite a case of 'do what you like' because there are obvious guidelines that *most* of us follow. I emphasise 'most' because there will always be disagreements between growers about which is the best way to germinate seed. One point to remember is that most of us are amateurs, in the sense that we do not grow plants for a living and so most of us are content to grow enough plants for our own use plus a few extra to give away or sell at plant sales. Nurserymen and other professionals need to get as near 100% germination as possible and that often requires a bit more care and attention.

Other authors have written on how to collect seed and I will start from the point when you have the packet in your hand, no matter whether it is your own or from somewhere else. The first problem is when to sow it. This is going to vary depending on the seed in question. There are many families and genera that germinate much better if they are sown fresh. The buttercup family is a good example. Germination of hellebores, for example, is erratic if sown in the spring but they come up like mustard and cress if sown as soon as they are dispersed. Pulsatillas respond in the same way. The same is true of the *Primula* family, including cyclamen, and many *Asteraceae* (*Compositae*) do better as well. Reference books will tell you which to sow when but there is doubt about many. The way to overcome this is to divide the packet into two, sow one half in the autumn and the other in spring.

This is all very well if you have the seed in the autumn but many of us acquire seed from seed exchanges or commercial sources which do not deliver until after the new year. Once the turn of the year has passed, my advice is to sow all the seed as soon as you get it – I am of course talking about sowing in pots not in the open ground.

The next thing to consider is what to sow the seed in. The traditional method illustrated in most gardening books is to sow your seed in trays. This is totally unnecessary unless you want a great number of plants. Most perennials are planted in groups of five or less (occasionally more). Allowing for a few to be a bit 'iffy' and perhaps a few to die and allowing for some to give away or sell, a dozen plants are sufficient for most of us. If the seed is of a rare plant then to a certain extent you are in honour bound to germinate it all and distribute the plants to others but for most purposes a dozen will do. If you do grow more then you not only have the expense of the extra compost and pots required but you also have to have space to keep them and the time to look after them.

Trays are out. On the whole a 9cm (3½in) pot is sufficient and in many cases even a 7.5cm (3in) will do. For large seed a larger half pot is better so that the seed can be sown well separated. For larger quantities of seed use a large half-litre pot or two or more smaller pots.

Compost is the next consideration and here you will find a great divergence of opinion. I know many growers who avidly swear by soil-less compost while other equally good growers will touch nothing but loam-based ones. Again, I feel it often has more to do with the gardener and the way he works than with the seed.

I personally always use a loam-based medium; I have never managed to grow successfully with soil-less ones. Loam-based composts drain more freely and yet retain sufficient moisture. It is difficult to over-water them – a great advantage as seed and seedlings do not like swampy conditions. If the pot dries out it is easy to re-wet. Soil-less compost, on the other hand, can easily be over-watered and yet, perversely, once dried out can be the very devil to re-wet – the water seems to pour away down the side of the pot, leaving the compost untouched. Soil-based composts are much better for seed that may take more than one season to germinate.

As far as the seed is concerned it does not seem to worry about what it germinates in – witness the aforementioned bench sweepings. In fact, germinating seed does not require very much. It has its own food supply and, as long as it gets moisture and light, its only requirement of the growing medium is as a place to put its roots to hold itself upright. The compost is very little more than a physical support. By way of an illustration, I am sure you have all grown mustard and cress on damp kitchen paper. Once the seedling develops it needs food and other nutrients. If the seedlings are transplanted soon after germination then, to a certain extent, the medium is irrelevant. If you are likely to be too

Linum perenne   **Sue Ward**

busy to prick them out straight away then the compost should contain some semblance of food and, indeed, most commercial sowing composts do. Loam-based composts have a certain amount of natural fertiliser in them and will therefore feed seedlings if transplanting is delayed.

Experiment and see which compost is the best for your way of working. There are plenty of commercial ones to choose from. Many of us still make our own and there are plenty of good reference works that will help you with this. Do not listen to fanatics, at least not until you are well experienced in growing. Composts made up with bull's blood, donkey's urine and sheep dung are not for the novice although there are still plenty of people who swear by such concoctions for their prize plants. Stick to the tried and tested and experiment later when you have experience.

Before you do anything else make out a label. This is so basic and yet how often do we forget, only to be confronted with a bench of identical pots with no idea what is in each? Another habit is to tear open the packet in such a way as to be unable to read the name on it! I like to put the name of the plant on the front of the label with the date of sowing across the top. On the reverse I usually make a note of the source of the seed in case something interesting occurs and I need to go back to the supplier. If, for example, it is HPS seed I simply note HPS, the year and the number on the seed list. If you are experimenting, you can also include information as to the compost used and various other details, but if you are this organised this type of information is better kept in a special notebook.

Put the label to one side and loosely fill the pot to the brim with your chosen medium and tap the pot to settle it. Do not ram it down into the pot. If you feel it has not settled enough, just lightly press it down with the base of another pot. The final level should be about the middle of the rim at the top of the pot. Watered a couple of times the surface of the compost will be roughly level with the bottom of the rim.

Sprinkle the seed thinly and evenly across the compost. If there is masses of seed in the packet do not be tempted to sow it all – give it away or throw it away. Large seeds can be sown singly across the surface to make certain that they are spread out. With some big seed, peonies for example, I am inclined to sow them into individual pots to save pricking them out.

The next stage is to cover the seed with a layer of grit. The old 'horticultural' grit was the ideal size (4mm) but this is difficult to find and the equivalent gravel is a bit too large. I use a chick grit obtainable from pet shops which supply it for chicken runs. It is perfect although a little on the expensive side – if you can get it in bags from an agricultural merchant it is much cheaper.

In more traditional books they still tell you to sift compost over the seeds but this has long gone out of favour with the vast majority of growers. When watered the fine compost frequently makes a hard pan on the surface so that water runs off and down the side of the pot. Grit allows water to percolate evenly through the compost. It also allows air in much more readily than a hard crust of fine compost. Another benefit is that it also holds the seed in place, whereas fine compost often gets washed to one side taking the seed with it. If the seed is to remain outside for a year or more grit helps prevent the rain compacting the top of the compost and also makes the removal of any weeds, moss or algae much easier. There might be the objection that those seeds that need light to germinate do not get it. In fact, the flinty grit allows more than enough light to percolate through.

I do not sow very fine seed directly onto the compost but sprinkle it on top of the grit and then use a watering can with a fine rose so that it is washed down between the pieces of grit.

If you have not already done so, put the label in before you do anything else. It is now time to water the pot. Some growers like to stand the pot in a bath or tray of water so that the compost is watered from below. This prevents the compost compacting and makes certain that it is wetted through. As soon as the surface changes colour take it out of the water. If you use a watering can, start your pass away from the pot so that the initial spurt has finished and only a fine spray descends on the grit.

Where to put the seed to germinate? The majority of perennial seed does not need warmth to germinate or, at least, not warmth from a propagator. As we have already seen violas will germinate in the refrigerator. However, if you are in a desperate hurry then a propagator will often speed up germination but there are only a very few cases where this is necessary. I germinate up to 300 pots of seed a year and never use the propagator which I reserve for cuttings.

I stand all my pots out in the open from the moment I sow them until I prick them out. They stand in an open cold frame whatever the weather. If we get a period of continual rain then I might put a light over them, leaving it propped open to allow air in. The majority of seedlings can be left where they are until you prick them out but some that germinate during warmer spells appreciate being put into a closed frame should the weather turn frosty again. The pots should not be in direct sunlight but those that have germinated should not be under trees or in dense shade or the seedlings will get drawn.

Not all seed will germinate in the first spring; some will require at least a year and some longer. I normally save any ungerminated pots for three years. I remember one pot I left for three years with nothing happening and then in the fourth a mass of seedlings burst through in a matter of a couple of days. They had all evidently been waiting for some trigger.

The only subject left uncovered is that of breaking dormancy. The majority of perennials that are reluctant to germinate can be encouraged to do so by a period of chilling. If sown in winter or early spring, the ambient temperature is usually sufficient to do this. If you keep your pots under cover or put them into a propagator then it may be necessary to put many of them in the refrigerator for at least three weeks.

Others need different techniques, some quite individual to the plant. I remember John Watson, who spends much of his time collecting wild seed in South America, telling me of the time he had taken sorting wild-collected alstroemeria seed as a large proportion of it seemed to have insect holes in it. Some time later, quite independently, Peter Thompson told me that they had discovered at the seed bank at Kew that the best way to germinate the more difficult alstroemeria was to make a small hole in the seed. What John had been throwing away was the very seed he should have kept; it was not damaged but had had its dormancy broken naturally by native insects – something Peter had discovered, as far as I remember, by trial and error based on experience.

On the whole though for the perennial gardener, chilling covers most ways of breaking dormancy. Occasionally the inhibiting factor is a hard seed case that needs to be softened and penetrated by spring rains before it will germinate. Sweet peas are a good example of this. If you just sow them they will eventually germinate but in order to get a more rapid and even germination many of the pea family should be soaked for a brief while in warm water. I recently read that soaking rots the seed so it is better to scarify either by shaking it in a bag with sharp sand or by attacking it with a knife or a file. As far as I know I have never suffered great losses through rotting so I will continue to soak them rather than the more tedious and dangerous methods of using knives or acid – as used to be recommended!

All those who succeed well with germination of difficult seed achieve their results by careful experiment based on what they feel are the natural conditions of the plant and its seed. However, it should be stressed that a large percentage of hardy perennials should present no problems if germinated using the methods described here.

I should just make a mention of sowing plants outside directly in the soil. Many hardy perennials are so accommodating that they can be sown in shallow drills outside in the spring just as the soil is warming up and left to their own devices. Attention is limited to ensuring that they are weeded and thinned out if necessary. Most should be ready to transplant by the autumn.

There is plenty more one can discover about breaking dormancy, or about other aspects of sowing seed for that matter, but this all tends to be for the specialist and far too detailed to go into here. I use the methods outlined here and I get more than adequate germination rates over a very wide range of plants, not only of those already in cultivation but also for seed received from the wild.

From Seedling to Flower

PETER THOMPSON

IT WOULD NOT SURPRISE ME if as many seedlings and small plants die i n the weeks following germination as are lost because seeds fail to germinate. Growing on is a critical time – and yet, how often one sees a school boy or girl, earning pocket money at the weekend, entrusted with the job of watering and hosing down the plants in a nursery. Watering is one of the most skilful aspects of gardening and something that cannot be taught in a day or two but has to be acquired by experience. Propagators are regarded as the specialists with the skills on which the production of plants depends but the skills of those who grow them on are often underrated. Knowing when and how much to feed, when to pot and repot, when to water or withhold water, day in day out, are crucial factors that make the difference between a plant thriving and merely existing until eventually deficiencies are revealed by its death.

Many amateur gardeners are people whose busy lives and other interests mean that they cannot be at home at all times. It is a mistake for them to attempt to follow commercial methods of growing plants, which tend to rely on somebody being available to keep an eye on things, combined with automated techniques requiring expensive equipment which you and I probably do not have and which our needs would never justify. When buying a shrub in a container we easily overlook the fact that it started off, possibly three years earlier, as a cutting. After producing roots it would have been potted up as a liner, grown on and moved into a one-litre pot. Later, months before we bought it, it would have been potted up again – this time into a three-litre pot. Every single day throughout those three years that shrub would have had some attention given to it even if it was no more than a passive check that all was well. Very few of us can be sure of being able to pot up, feed, water and generally look after plants daily for three or four years, so we need to find other less demanding ways to raise our plants. A good starting point is equipment, and we can then go on to look at the care of seedlings and processes like pricking out, potting up and growing on.

EQUIPMENT

A greenhouse is one of the most effective tools at the propagator's disposal but a cold greenhouse, though it will cost a great deal more, will be of very little more use to you than a cold frame. The big difference is that you can walk into a greenhouse and experience precisely the conditions inside it, and in the winter in particular it is much more tempting to nip into the greenhouse than spend time lifting frame lights to see how things are going. So the plants are likely to be better looked after in the greenhouse. Problems will be spotted quicker. For example, given the chance field mice graze my plants in the winter like little cows and if I leave my plants unchecked for a fortnight or so, it is all too likely that they will be simply eaten away. I am more likely to spot the problem early in a greenhouse than a cold frame.

If a greenhouse is worth buying at all, it is always worth spending a bit more to heat it economically and with regard to what is to be grown in it. In a propagating house used for hardy, or even slightly tender, plants, that need not be an expensive business. Warmed air may comfort the gardener but, when the plants occupy only a small part of the house, it does them little good and it is extremely expensive. So I heat only the benches, using heating cables set out on grids of heavy gauge wire (such as weldmesh) to keep them in place, embedded in a layer of fine grit or sand 7.5-10cm (3-4in) deep, covering the benches. The heat input is controlled through a thermostat, and on cold nights, and even during the days when the cold persists, the plants on the bench are covered with a blanket of bubble polythene to keep the heat in. The result is that the only part of the greenhouse which is heated is the part that actually contains plants and, depending on the setting of the thermostat and the stage of development of the plants, this may be 15 °C, or even 20°C, or only a few degrees above freezing point.

Hardy perennials grown from seed sown fresh from the capsules during the summer require very little heat during the winter. Some germinate within weeks of being sown, others emerge months later during the winter or early the following spring. I seldom prick out or pot up any before the winter. They may fail to establish themselves in their new pots and then die while they occupy so much more space than when crowded together. Even though they are hardy and would probably survive out of doors, these seedlings benefit a great deal from being on a greenhouse bench where temperatures are prevented from falling below freezing point. Rather than heat all the benches in a greenhouse by a single long cable, I prefer to install several separate systems, so that there is a choice of different temperature régimes to suit plants with different needs. If plants that need high temperatures are being grown, two heating cables can be installed in the same area, one 2-3cm (¾-1½in) above the other – rather like a two-bar electric fire – and either one or both switched on depending how cold it is. The bubble polythene used to protect the plants on cold nights can simply be placed on top of the plants without doing any permanent harm. Alternatively I construct a tunnel out of stock wire which provides a frame on which the polythene rests well above the plants themselves.

Electric lamps designed to supplement light during the winter are invaluable for propagating or growing on. At 150 watts per bulb these are effective and reasonably economical, provided they are used carefully. Rather than using them to extend the day length the plants will benefit most when they are switched on daily for a few hours either side of midday so that they augment whatever natural light there may be. Much more economical, but one of the most practical and effective investments I have made is a fan to circulate the air – a small 15-watt unit keeps the air moving in a modest-sized greenhouse, and entirely prevents the stale, dank feeling that leads inevitably to the onset of moulds during the dull, dark days of midwinter. Once the dark days are over it is no longer needed.

My use of bubble polythene is not confined to the greenhouse. I always use it to 'glaze' my cold frames. Glass, with its weight, its vulnerability to breakage and its sharp edges when broken, is a nightmare on a frame, especially with children around. Bubble polythene not only avoids these problems but also diffuses light, removing much of its heat and providing a kinder atmosphere for the growth of plants, especially seedlings and cuttings, than a traditionally glazed frame.

PLANTS

An account of sowing seeds appears elsewhere in this booklet but, as with so many things in gardening, there are different ways to achieve the same objective and since my way is quite different from other methods I think it is worth offering it as an alternative. I use small square plastic pots, 7 or 9cm (3-4in), which I first fill to within about 3cm (1in) of the top with potting compost. These are topped up with vermiculite, or a material called Seramis which has recently become available and which is a baked clay mineral looking like rounded fragments of crushed bricks. It is porous and acts as a very open, but not sharp, grit providing conditions which many seeds find congenial for the production of seedlings. Tiny seeds, such as foxgloves, lady's mantle or lobelias, are sown by sprinkling them over the surface and watering them in. Seeds about the size of a pin head, such as columbines, delphiniums or dianthus, should be sown on the surface and lightly covered by ploughing them in using a pointed dibber. Large, or awkwardly shaped, seeds are sown on a thin layer of Seramis or vermiculite and then covered with a deeper layer to fill the pot. This system has consistently given me good results. The well-aerated, moist but not saturated conditions of the mineral topping (vermiculite or Seramis) discourage the onset of damping off and prevent the problems caused by under or over watering that make peat composts so difficult to manage. The upper layer in which seeds are sown contains no nutrients, but once the seeds germinate their roots penetrate to the potting compost below where they obtain the nutrients they need until they are ready to prick out.

The rule about pricking out is to do it as soon as the seed leaves have expanded fully. That might sound rather challenging – especially with plants that produce minute seedlings – but even with something as microscopic as a foxglove it is better done sooner rather than later. The tiniest seedlings prove quite easy to handle once the attempt is made. In prospect, they look so fragile that it seems impossible to handle them without doing irrevocable damage. In fact, it is the roots that are the most vulnerable to damage and these develop so rapidly that if pricking out is delayed until the true leaves appear they may already be so extensive that they cannot be moved without damage.

Salesmen propagate the myth that degradable peat or paper pots are beneficial because they avoid disturbing the roots when planting out. But there is no reason why the roots should suffer – anyone can knock a plant out of a pot without damaging it. All you need do is turn the pot upside-down, keeping two fingers over the top to prevent the contents tumbling out, and give it a tap on the bottom. The plant and the compost slide out together ready to pot up, plant out or be done with as you will. The first try may be a disaster but it is an easy knack to acquire and when done the roots of the plant are exposed ready to grow straight out into their new surroundings. In a peat pot, on the other hand, the roots must first make their way through the peat itself and if that dries out it can be an almost impenetrable barrier – and it is very likely to dry out because the rim of the pot above the surface acts as a wick drawing water out of the peat below. A further drawback is that these expendable pots must be renewed every year, adding up to an expensive option, whereas well made plastic pots will do service for many years.

The seeds of most hardy perennials germinate best at low or moderate temperatures and many require periods of exposure close to freezing-point before they produce seedlings. But some, including hostas, germinate most rapidly and completely at unexpectedly high temperatures. At 25 °C seedlings will emerge within about ten days; at lower temperatures they take much longer – up to three or four months at 10 °C. These can grow into large plants which most of us need in comparatively small numbers, so pricking them out into a seed tray holding fifty or sixty seedlings would be quite inappropriate. Instead try pricking out into 9cm (3½in) square pots, putting five seedlings in each pot, one in each corner and one in the centre. Any number of pots can be filled depending on how many plants are needed, providing a convenient, flexible unit with the added advantage of greater depth than any seed tray and in which roots have more freedom to develop.

Alstroemerias represent another group of plants for which high temperatures play an essential part in germination. In this case temperatures of about 25 °C do not lead directly to germination but enable the seeds to germinate later at temperatures below 10 °C. Timing is critical because soon after midsummer these plants tend to die down and seedlings need time to grow big enough to produce storage rhizomes before this happens. Ideally the seeds should be sown in January and kept for about six weeks at high temperatures. The simplest way is to mix them with damp vermiculite contained in a plastic sandwich box with a close fitting lid which is put into the airing cupboard. After six weeks the box containing the seeds is transferred to cooler temperatures – around the end of February/beginning of March a cold frame provides the right conditions. Once the seeds start to germinate they can be potted individually into small pots (7cm/3in) and will grow on steadily till they start to go dormant in late summer.

Hygiene rules our lives today – many people even devote their precious gardening time to washing pots! But stories abound of unregenerate gardeners whose potting sheds are a disgrace; places where old potting compost and new are mixed together, and yet the results are phenomenally successful. It may be though that muckiness brings its own reward and that not all plants appreciate our concern with hygiene. When trying to grow the burning bush (*Dictamnus albus*), I have found it is not particularly difficult to germinate but very difficult to grow on. The seedlings emerge, they remain static and, by the end of summer, life obviously has not fulfilled their expectations and they fade quietly away. Obviously something is missing from their lives. This applies to quite a number of interesting plants. It does not apply to hostas; hostas are very obliging, as you can tell from the enormous number of hosta seedlings and cultivars at our disposal. Anyone can grow a hosta, but not everyone can grow a dictamnus.

At Kew large numbers of plants were collected for the Seed Bank amongst which were many clovers and other members of the pea family. These were dutifully chipped to damage their seed coats so that water could reach their embryos and most germinated readily. Then things started to go wrong. They stopped growing and almost without exception turned yellow, withered away and died despite having nutrients lavished on them to try to keep them alive. Eventually we found that the answer was to mix small amounts of unsterilised soil from a field with the potting compost in which the seeds were sown. This provided a source of nitrogen-fixing bacteria which congregated in nodules on the plants' roots in a symbiotic association through which the plants obtained the nitrogen they depended on for survival. A great many symbiotic relationships exist between plants and bacteria, and plants and fungi – the most familiar involve nitrogen fixation, but others enable plants to make use of otherwise insoluble forms of phosphorous and perhaps other nutrients. Plants potted up in sterile (hygienic) composts cannot form these associations and this is one of the reasons that some plants, dictamnus perhaps, which we label as difficult, fail to thrive.

When plants are grown commercially a stage is reached some time after seeds have been sown or cuttings taken when they are put into containers to grow until large enough to sell. At this point many amateur gardeners would do well to forget about growing plants in containers but look instead at the much less demanding methods based on growing plants in the ground. If your garden is such that small plants would be too much at risk planted straight out into their permanent positions, a nursery bed provides a practical alternative. Part-time gardeners could use nursery beds a great deal more than they do. All that is needed is a reasonably sheltered site, preferably supplied with water, that can be dug over and prepared to the standard of a vegetable patch in which small plants are set out in rows and left to develop into big plants. That is how they used to be grown in nurseries but, being familiar only with container-grown plants, many people have become fearful of digging up and transplanting though, when done carefully, especially in the winter, the chances of successful re-establishment are better than when planting out from containers. The great advantage of a nursery bed is that the burden of constant attention on which container grown plants depend is avoided; the disadvantage is that plants not used in due time may grow too big so that, whether the plants are needed or not, occasional clearances are an essential part of management.

I should like to end with a question. Under natural conditions many plants display strong preferences for the soils in which they grow, a fact which gardeners by and large tend to ignore. We know that some plants, rhododendrons amongst them, are calcifuge but our awareness more or less stops there. Foresters, more aware of these differences, recognise, for example, that the seeds of giant redwoods germinate on mineral-based soils, while western hemlocks produce seedlings only on humus-rich soils – corresponding respectively to loam-based and peat-based composts. These differences distinguish pioneer species like the redwoods, that colonise newly exposed ground often after fires, from settler species like hemlocks, which infiltrate established communities. Numerous plants, including perennials, play the roles of pioneer or settler but, so far as I know, gardeners have paid scarcely any attention to these roles at all. Could it be that our failure to take account of these fundamental differences is one reason that we find some plants so amenable in cultivation but others so reluctant?

The Benefits of Sowing Fresh Seed

TIM INGRAM

ALTHOUGH THERE ARE MANY SPECIES OF PLANTS which produce seed of short viability, in relatively few is this so limited that they must be sown absolutely fresh. These include woody plants such as willow and poplar (whose seed has very thin protective coat) and oak, chestnut and beech (whose nut-like seeds must be kept moist). Among herbaceous plants the most notable examples are *Corydalis*, certain primulas and early-flowering woodland genera, such as *Epimedium*, *Hacquetia*, *Hepatica*, *Jeffersonia*, *Shortia* and *Trillium*. Germination of many other species, however, is greatly enhanced if their seed is sown soon after collection in the summer and autumn. Good examples are *Astrantia*, *Cyclamen*, *Gentiana*, *Helleborus* and *Pulsatilla*. A number of these seeds lay down their food reserves in the form of oils and fats rather than carbohydrates, and become progressively more hydrophobic as they dry out. Improved germination of older seed, cyclamen and hellebores for example, may be achieved by soaking in warm water prior to sowing.

Even for those plants whose seed will retain its viability for many years (under optimum storage) early sowing will often result in germination more quickly and uniformly than from stored seed. This is especially true of plants such as peonies and some lilies (see below) which may require more than one alternating cycle of high and low temperatures to complete germination. Conversely there are many plants, typically from mediterranean climates, whose seed requires a dry after-ripening period before germination can proceed. Seed of such plants classically germinates quickly in warm moist conditions and is best sown in the spring.

The dormancy of seeds only develops as they begin to mature and dry off. If seed is sown before it is fully ripe, it may be possible to obtain very rapid germination in otherwise very recalcitrant plants such as acers, viburnums and many of the Rosaceae. The seed of certain primulas is sometimes sown 'in the green' but similar treatment of other herbaceous plants has not been examined as far as I am aware.

You may think that the seeds to lose their viability most quickly would be those which are very small, such as the minute seed of orchids or spores of ferns. Some fern spores do lose viability very quickly – the royal fern (*Osmunda regalis*) has green spores which must be sown within a week or two of collection – but most will survive for several years if carefully stored and spores of tree ferns have successfully germinated after 10-15 years. Orchid seed too can retain its viability for a considerable time before it encounters a suitable fungal partner to enable germination.

As you begin to study those seeds which need to be sown fresh it is notable that a large number of woodland plants comes in this category. They also tend to be associated with particular plant families. Prominent

Anemone multifida   **Sue Ward**

among these is the *Ranunculaceae* and others include the closely related *Berberidaceae, Fumariaceae, Gentianaceae, Rosaceae, Saxifragaceae* and *Apiaceae (Umbelliferae)*. In some of these plants, for example *Anemone nemorosa* and tuberous species of *Corydalis*, the seed embryo is only poorly differentiated at the time the seed is shed and requires a warm moist environment during spring and summer to develop fully and allow germination to occur. For these, and other woodland gems such as *Hepatica* and *Jeffersonia*, the seed rapidly loses viability as it dries out and is best sown immediately after collection. Limited storage may be effected by keeping the seed sealed in plastic envelopes with a little damp vermiculite or peat, and such a method would facilitate distribution of seed in the summer.

With all these plants it pays to keep a close check on the seed as it matures and collect it promptly as it ripens. The seed (or achenes) of *Hepatica* and *Anemone* turn from green to yellow-brown and can be gently rubbed off the flower stalk when ripe. In *Jeffersonia* the pods turn creamy-yellow and split open to reveal the glossy plump brown seed. As this lies beneath the canopy of fresh new foliage, a close eye is needed to catch the seed before it is carried away by ants, which are attracted to an oily appendage (or elaiosome). The seeds of *Corydalis* and *Dicentra* have a similar fatty appendage and are best collected while the pods are still green, after gently testing to see if they will split open.

Although it is important to sow fresh seed of these plants, they will rarely germinate before the following winter or spring. As Peter Thompson has said, 'Many plants have developed mechanisms which enable them first of all to ignore the present and to forecast the future, and then to measure the passage of time and to verify the advent and passing of winter.' Almost invariably, germination of such species occurs at the same time that the parent plant begins to grow, suggesting that a common mechanism links the breaking of dormancy of the mature plant and of the seed. Hellebores, of course, start growing very early in the year; they are among the earliest flowering of woodland perennials, and freshly-sown hellebore seed frequently germinates in the late autumn or early winter. Many species of *Cyclamen* have the fascinating property of ripening their seed at about the same time, midsummer, even though they flower at quite different times of the year – freshly-sown seed will then germinate according to the time of year that the parent plant normally produces its foliage. We sow fresh seed of the lovely European woodland umbellifer *Hacquetia epipactis* in early summer each year and obtain superb germination the following March, and similar results are obtained from good forms of *Astrantia major*, such as 'Ruby Wedding'.

Another most unusual group of umbellifers is the New Zealand spear-grasses, or *Aciphylla*. Seed has been recently introduced directly when ripe (late in the New Zealand summer) and sown in March or April in the UK. Generally germination has been very good, though usually not until the following spring. Subsequent development of the young seedlings of *Aciphylla* and other New Zealand genera such as *Celmisia* can be painfully slow and it is wise to allow sturdy young plants to develop before potting them on individually. A requirement for fresh seed seems to be generally true of much of the flora of New Zealand, Tasmania and temperate South America and may relate to the relatively cool, moist climate of these regions.

Most of the plants I have discussed so far have been woodland perennials. These flower early in the year and set seed by midsummer, a time when conditions are not conducive to good seedling establishment. The evolution of mechanisms to delay germination until the autumn or, more often, the following spring is essential for their survival. The same requirement, though in a rather different environment, is true of many alpine species. Although fewer of these plants show a large drop in viability of their stored seed, the advantage of sowing in the autumn comes from providing the seed with conditions as close as possible to those they experience in nature. Following a warm moist autumn and long cold winter, germination of many alpine species can be excellent. Seed sown in winter or early spring will often only germinate erratically or after another autumn/winter cycle.

This is even truer of those plants whose seed may require several alternating cycles of warm and cold conditions before germination is complete. In extreme cases, seed of genera such as *Iris* and *Trillium* have been known to germinate freely five or six years after sowing! A number of such plants show germination of the radicle (seedling root) but the embryonic shoot remains dormant until the seed has experienced a significant cold period, i.e. winter. Good examples are found in the two genera *Lilium* and *Paeonia*. Older seed may show a double dormancy, with the root requiring a warm period and the shoot one or more successive cold cycles. Hence full germination may take from six months to eighteen months or longer. It is fascinating, and disconcerting, to look at pots of peony seed and see vigorous roots appearing through the drainage holes with nary a sign of any shoot growth! Several years ago I was given 150 or so seeds of *Paeonia cambessedesii* and sowed them fresh in the autumn. I was so disappointed by the meagre germination of sixteen seedlings the following spring that I couldn't be bothered to prick them out. They were left in the tray and forgotten. After a year of neglect virtually every other seed germinated the following spring. I have had similar experience with the giant lily, *Cardiocrinum giganteum*.

The lilies show a range of germination patterns: some, such as *L. regale* and *L. candidum*, will appear quickly after sowing (at 15-20 °C); others, such as *L. martagon* and *L. monadelphum*, show dormancy of the embryonic shoot and require a period of cold. With the latter, final germination can be hastened by giving the moist seed (in sealed polythene bags) artificial periods of warmth (18-21 °C for twelve weeks) and cool conditions (4 °C for six weeks). This is particularly helpful with seed not obtained early enough in the autumn for normal sowing. Although not sharing the same mechanism as lilies, alstroemerias also require a warm/cold cycle to initiate germination, and this pattern is clearly quite common among plants, relating as it does to the ambient conditions of autumn and winter.

Some seed, however, is shy to germinate even when sown fresh and allowed to experience the normal cycles of nature. Over several years I have sown *Sanguinaria canadensis* and *Tropaeolum speciosum* and obtained only very limited germination, if any at all. Possibly such seed requires significantly colder and longer winters than we normally experience in the south of England. Certainly it is noticeable that germination of many species is greatly increased following severe winters, particularly with snow cover. A fridge for stratifying moist sown seed and, incidentally, for storing dry seed may therefore prove essential for the committed seed-sower.

The length of time between sowing and germination of many of the plants I have mentioned clearly increases potential losses from predation and/or severe weather. I find a well-drained soil-based seed compost, such as John Innes, with extra grit or perlite, most suitable. The seeds are routinely covered with 5mm (¹/₅in) of chick or aquarium grit, washed free of fine particles, to protect them from heavy rain and desiccation. A thinner covering is given to those few species which require light for germination, such as *Digitalis* and *Gentiana*. Generally pots are kept in an open but mouse-proof frame (with 10mm/²/₅in wire-mesh) in light shade, watered in dry spells and covered with glass lights when the rain is extremely heavy or the conditions very severe. Following germination, pots are routinely transferred to the warmer, protected conditions of the greenhouse.

Allied with the benefits of sowing many seeds fresh in the summer and autumn comes the enjoyment of collecting your own seed in the garden, as discussed earlier. The satisfaction of obtaining successful germination of *Jeffersonia* and *Glaucidium* and many more humble species can be renewed year after year and along the way we learn that plants will always have more to teach us.

Aquilegia vulgaris **Sue Ward**

Further Reading

BOOKS

Bird, R. (1993). *The Propagation of Hardy Perennials*. Batsford, London.

Bradbeer, J.W. (1994). *Seed Dormancy and Germination*. A. & P. Blackie, Glasgow

Deno, N.C. (1993). *Seed Germination Theory and Practice*. Published by the author. Available from the Alpine Garden Society at the AGS Centre, Avon Bank, Pershore, Worcs. WR10 3JP.

Gardiner, J. (1997). *Propagation from Seed: A Wisley Handbook*. The RHS, London.

Harkness, M.G. (1993). 2nd ed. *The Bernard E. Harkness Seedlist Handbook*. Batsford, London.

Kelly, J. (1996). *Growing Plants from Seed*. Ward Lock, London.

Lloyd, C. & Rice, G. (1991). *Garden Flowers from Seed*. Viking, London.

Platt, K. (1997). *The Seed Search*. Available from the compiler/editor at 37 Melbourne Rd., Crooks, Sheffield SR10 1NR.

Salisbury, E.J. (1946). *Seeds and their Germination in the Living Garden*. G. Bell & Sons Ltd., London.

Sharman, J. (1992). *Plant Cultivars Coming True from Seed*. Available from the author at Monksilver Nursery, Oakington Rd., Cottenham, Cambs. CB4 4TW.

Thompson, P. (1992). *Creative Propagation: A Grower's Guide*. Batsford, London.

Young, J.A. & Young, C.C. (1986). *Collecting, Processing and Germinating Seeds of Wildland Plants*. Timber Press, Cambridge.

PERIODICALS

Bird, R. (ed.). (1987-91). *Growing from Seed*. Quarterly journals of Thompson & Morgan, Ipswich.

Charlesworth, G. (1992). 'Looking at Seed.' *Bull. Amer. Rock Gdn. Soc.*, 50, 186.

Good, J.E. (1974). 'Rock Garden Plants from Seed.' *Bull. Alpine Gdn. Soc.*, 42, 135, 239 & 319.

Good, J.E. (1975). 'Rock Garden Plants from Seed.' *Bull. Alpine Gdn. Soc.*, 43, 69, 153 & 246.

Jelitto, K. (1989). 'Seed Germination.' *Bull. Amer. Rock Gdn. Soc.*, 47, 33.

Klingaman, G. (1989). 'A Look at Seed Viability.' *Bull. Amer. Rock Gdn. Soc.*, 47, 184.